THE
TUDORS & STUARTS

Philip Sauvain

Wayland

Look into the Past

The Ancient Chinese
The Anglo-Saxons
The Aztecs
The Egyptians
The Greeks
The Incas
The Japanese
The Maya
The Normans
The Romans
The Sioux
The Tudors & Stuarts
The Victorians
The Vikings

Series editor: Joanna Bentley
Series designer: David West
Book designer: Joyce Chester

First published in 1995 by Wayland (Publishers) Limited,
61 Western Road, Hove, East Sussex, BN3 1JD, England

British Library Cataloguing in Publication Data
  Sauvain, Philip
  Tudors & Stuarts.–(Look into the Past series)
  I. Title II. Series
  942.05

ISBN 0 7502 1213 6

Typeset by Dorchester Typesetting Group Ltd., Dorset,
England.
Printed and bound in Italy by L.E.G.O. S.p.A., Vicenza,
Italy.

Picture acknowledgements
The publishers wish to thank the following for providing the
pictures in this book: Bridgeman Art Library 5 (top left and
right), 7 (bottom), 9 (bottom), 25 (both, top by courtesy of
the Marquess of Salisbury), 26, 27 (bottom left and right), 29
(top); British Library 20; Cambridge University Library 27
(top); E T Archive 6, 8, 13 (bottom); Fitzwilliam Museum,
University of Cambridge 15 (bottom), 24; Fotomas Index 5
(bottom right), 7 (top), 9 (top), 22 (left), 29 (bottom); Philip
Sauvain 11 (bottom), 12, 13 (top left and right), 14, 15 (top),
16, 17 (bottom) 18, 19 (bottom), 22 (right), 23 (all), 28
(both); Wayland Picture Library 10, 19 (top left and right,
Museum of London), 20. Family tree on page 4 by Joyce
Chester.

CONTENTS

Words that appear in **_bold italic_** in the text are explained in the glossary on page 30.

TUDOR AND STUART MONARCHS

The Tudors and Stuarts were the kings and queens who reigned in Britain from 1485 to 1714. Henry Tudor, grandson of Owen Tudor of Wales, became King Henry VII when he defeated and killed Richard III at the Battle of Bosworth Field in 1485. This victory and his marriage to Elizabeth of York helped to end the Wars of the Roses between the rival royal families of York and Lancaster.

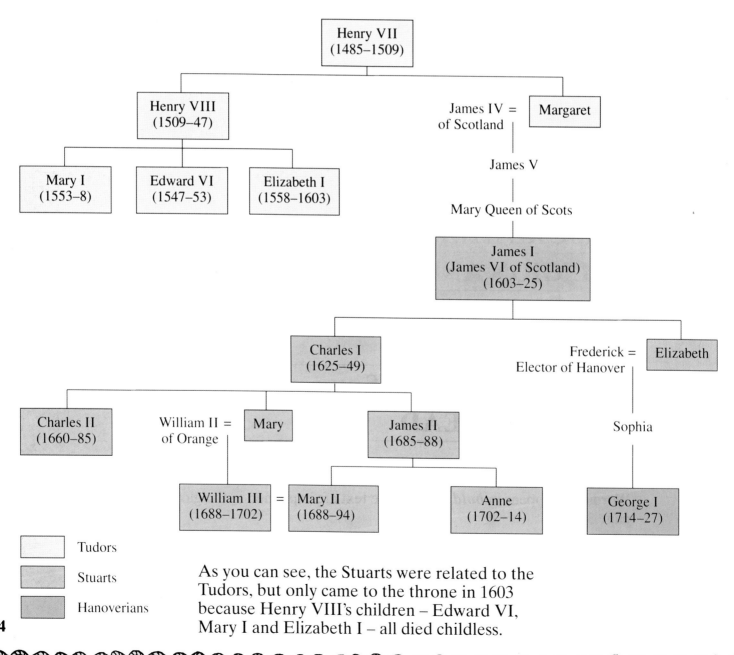

Tudors

Stuarts

Hanoverians

As you can see, the Stuarts were related to the Tudors, but only came to the throne in 1603 because Henry VIII's children – Edward VI, Mary I and Elizabeth I – all died childless.

▲ Charles I became the second Stuart king in 1625. He tried to rule without the support of Parliament and this led to the English *Civil War* and his trial and execution in 1649.

▲ Henry VIII badly wanted a son to follow him as king. His first wife, Catherine of Aragon, gave birth to several children but only Mary survived. When Henry divorced Catherine and married Anne Boleyn, he broke away from the Roman Catholic Church. This led in time to Britain turning *Protestant*. Anne Boleyn, who was later executed for treason, had a daughter Elizabeth but this was not good enough for Henry. Then in 1537 his third wife, Jane Seymour, gave him Edward, the son he wanted, although she died eighteen days later. Henry had three more wives, but no further children.

Oliver Cromwell, a ▶ strong Protestant, fought for Parliament against the king in the Civil War. He seized power himself in 1653 and ruled Britain as *Lord Protector*. His strict *Puritan* supporters made life so hard for people that they welcomed the return of King Charles II after Cromwell died.

CLOTHES AND FASHIONS

The Puritans wore black clothes with stiff, white linen collars. They thought that wearing bright colours was sinful. Poor people, too, wore plain, simple clothes made from coarse wool. Only the rich bought clothes made from cooler, lighter fabrics, such as muslin, satin or silk.

Paintings tell us about the clothes worn in the past. This one shows Sir Thomas More and members of his family in about 1530. Most are wearing long dark gowns and some have puffed-up collars around their necks called *ruffs*. ▼

In this painting Queen Elizabeth I is carried ▶ through the streets by admiring courtiers. Her ladies-in-waiting can be seen wearing huge ruffs and long silk or satin gowns drawn in tight at the waist. A hooped frame called a *farthingale* made their skirts spread out. The men wore tight-fitting jackets, called doublets, and padded hose (stockings pulled up to the waist).

Most Tudor and Stuart pictures are of rich people but this one, painted in 1670, shows the clothes worn by ordinary people as well. The owner of the mansion and his family (centre) are dressed in fine clothes. Their servants (left) carry baskets of food to give to the poor people of the village (right). ▼

EATING AND DRINKING

Poor people ate a simple diet of bread, cheese, broth (a type of soup) and sometimes meat. They drank a coarse type of beer called ale. Rich people ate huge meals with many different meats, such as mutton, beef, pork, bacon, veal, rabbit and venison (deer meat) as well as eggs, fish, fruit, vegetables, spices and bread. They also drank wine as well as ale.

The children of a noble lord enjoy the sweet course at dinner – fresh fruit (pears, apples, grapes) and nuts. The family pets on the table – a parrot and a monkey – show that Elizabethan sailors were already bringing exciting new products and animals to Britain, such as potatoes and tobacco from America.

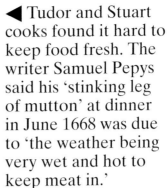

◄ Tudor and Stuart cooks found it hard to keep food fresh. The writer Samuel Pepys said his 'stinking leg of mutton' at dinner in June 1668 was due to 'the weather being very wet and hot to keep meat in.'

Coffee was first brought to Britain in 1641 and the first coffee houses opened in 1650. By 1700 there were 2,000 in London alone. Coffee houses were very popular with men, who went there to gossip and smoke a pipe of tobacco. There were other new drinks as well. In September 1660 Samuel Pepys had 'a cup of tee (a China drink) of which I never had drank before' and in November 1664 he went 'to a Coffee-house, to drink jocolatte, very good.'

▼

CARING FOR YOUNG AND OLD

Many almshouses were founded at this time. These were homes for old people who were no longer able to look after themselves. Rich men and women left money when they died to help pay for almshouses. They also left money to build schools. Many old towns in Britain have almshouses or old schools which were founded like this hundreds of years ago.

There were many beggars in the streets in Tudor and Stuart towns. They relied on charity to keep themselves alive. Some starved to death. A new law in 1601 made everyone pay a tax, called the poor-rate, to help the people in each parish who were unable to help themselves, such as the sick, aged and handicapped.

Most babies died before the age of one. All but one of Catherine of Aragon's five children died and, nearly two hundred years later, all five of Queen Anne's children died in infancy. Most of those who did survive were treated badly. They were whipped with a birch rod if they misbehaved or disobeyed their parents. Only rich children had many toys.

Few children went to school before 1500. In the Tudor and Stuart periods, however, many free grammar schools were founded for boys, such as the one shown here at Market Harborough in Leicestershire. ▶ The schoolroom was above the market hall. Rules at these grammar schools were very strict. Pupils were beaten if they disobeyed a rule, such as coming to school 'with dirty shoes or unwashed faces'.

LIVING IN LONDON

London was by far the largest city in Britain, with 500,000 inhabitants in 1660, compared with 30,000 in Norwich, the next largest town. Supplying Londoners with food and water and getting rid of their litter and sewage was a problem.

This map, drawn in 1591, shows that Tudor London was close to green fields. But the town was already growing fast and new homes were being built on the outskirts. Visitors complained about the noise of London's crowds, its thieves and pickpockets, and the smell of rotting rubbish in the streets. ▼

Over 100,000 Londoners died during the ▶ Great *Plague* in 1665-6. You can see the dead being taken away in coffins in these pictures. When people caught the disease, their homes were sealed off and a red cross on the door warned people to stay away. This couldn't stop the disease spreading since it was carried by black rats which thrived in summer on the refuse in London's streets.

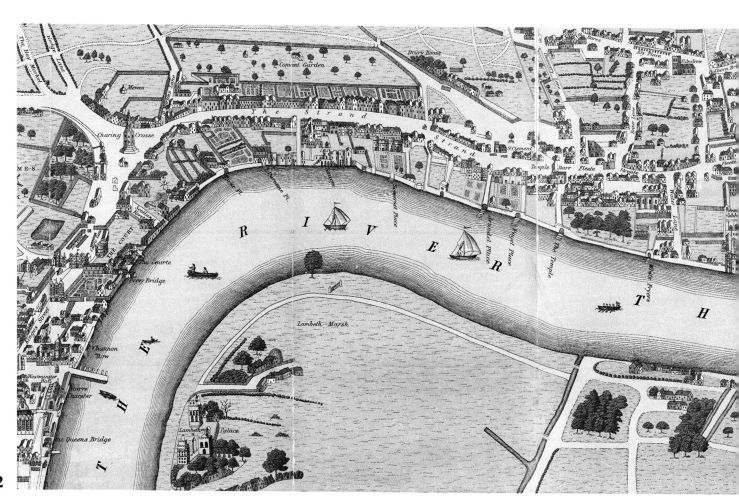

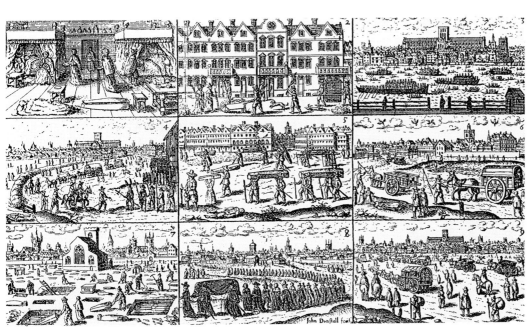

On Sunday, 2 September 1666, a great fire began in a baker's shop in Pudding Lane, near London Bridge. It soon spread rapidly. A hot, dry summer had made everything bone-dry and a fierce wind fanned the flames. Five days later, writer John Evelyn's shoes burned as he climbed over heaps of smoking rubbish. 'London was, but is no more,' he said. ▼

A plaque on the ▲ Monument to the Great Fire of London tells us it destroyed 13,200 houses, 400 streets, 89 churches and the old St Paul's Cathedral.

HOUSES AND HOMES

Few homes in 1500 were built of bricks or had glass windows. Most were made of wood. They were often built close to one another, with the upper storeys built on wooden beams (jetties) hanging over the rooms below. This made the streets dark since the upper storeys on both sides were very close to each other.

Smallhythe Place in Kent was built in about ▲ 1500. The walls of Tudor houses like this were made of thin strips of wood and plaster and built around a timber frame. They often had tall brick chimneys and small *mullioned windows* made up of many tiny panes of glass.

This is the royal palace at Richmond, near ▶ London, in 1620. Luxury homes had been built by then along the river Thames. Notice the different ways of travelling and the Morris dancers on the river bank.

The Duke's Head ▶
hotel in King's Lynn,
Norfolk, was built as a
private home in about
1689. Stuart buildings
at this time had doors
and windows on one
side exactly matching
those on the other.
There were alternate
long and square
stones (called *quoins*)
at the corners. They
also had sash windows
which slid up and
down and roofs
sloping at both ends
and at the sides.

TRAVEL AND TRADE

Roads in Tudor and Stuart Britain were terrible. Celia Fiennes said the surface of a narrow road near Bath was so bad, the wheels of her coach 'were once so wedged in the stones that several men were forced to lift us out.' It was fit only for packhorses, she said. These were the animals who carried packs of wool to seaports on the east coast facing Europe, such as London, Hull and Ipswich. After the discovery of America, however, ports on the west coast, such as Bristol, Liverpool and Glasgow, also began to thrive.

◄ This merchant ship was carved in the early 1500s, on the end of a wooden bench in Bishop Lydeard Church in Somerset. Ships like this brought spices, silk, tea, cotton and coffee to Britain from many parts of the world.

Trade with India ▲ and the Far East grew rapidly in Tudor and Stuart times as the voyages of explorers opened up the world. These ships belonged to the East India Company. The picture, painted in the seventeenth century, shows them setting out to sail down the coast of Africa and then across the Indian Ocean to the Company's trading stations in India.

Merchants had to pay taxes, called customs duties, on foreign goods brought into the country, such as wine and silk. The Customs House in King's Lynn was built on the quayside at the end of the seventeenth century. Nearby are the homes and warehouses of the merchants. ▶

SHOPS AND MARKETS

We know how people bought and sold food in Tudor and Stuart times from pictures painted at the time. The places where they shopped can be seen in many old towns, such as the market cross or market hall. Coins used by shopkeepers and their customers are sometimes dug up in gardens today. They usually carry an image of the king or queen, the date and the value of the coin.

This market place in Lavenham in Suffolk ▲ has a stepped market cross. The ledges were used by farmers to display their fruit, vegetables, eggs, butter and cheese. The small building on the right may have been the toll house where traders paid a small fee (called a toll) to sell their goods in the market square.

The Tudor shops in Lavenham in Suffolk ▶ have arched openings which were plastered over long ago. Early in the morning, 400 years ago, you would have seen the shopkeeper pulling down the hinged wooden shutters covering these openings at night. They acted as shop counters during the day.

Market traders sold fruit, fish, poultry, eggs and meat. Can you see what these two men have in their baskets? Traders like these would be seen in every town in Europe in Tudor and Stuart times.

LADY STREET

IN THE COUNTRY

Most people lived in the countryside. In many villages, the land was divided into long narrow strips in huge common fields without fences or hedges. By 1700, however, many poor farmers had lost their strips of land after landowners took them over and enclosed the fields with walls or hedges to rear sheep. Many unemployed farmers became beggars as a result.

▲ This farm was painted in about 1500. You can see the farmer hard at work, reaping the wheat.

◀ This country scene was painted in the seventeenth century and shows farm cottages and the long dykes which were dug to drain the land of water.

The flat fenland in eastern England used to be an area of marsh and water where people lived by hunting and fishing. By 1600, however, low-lying land like this in the Netherlands had been drained to grow crops. The Stuarts did the same in Britain. They dug huge drainage channels and built windmills to pump water from the land into these channels taking it to the sea. The newly-reclaimed land was used to graze livestock and later ploughed to grow crops.

21

INDUSTRY AND CRAFTS

Although there were no modern industries, towards the end of the Stuart period there were already signs of the changes to come. Over ten times as much coal was mined in 1700 compared with 1550. By 1714, Thomas Savery and Thomas Newcomen had invented steam pumps and Abraham Darby was already smelting iron ore with coke (from coal) instead of charcoal (from wood).

▲ Printing cheap books in the sixteenth century made it possible for people to know more about their world. Workplaces like this were among the first to use complicated machinery.

◀ This waterwheel was used to lift a heavy hammer at Wortley Forge, near Sheffield in Yorkshire. It hammered red-hot iron into shape. A stream of water was directed on to the blades of the waterwheel, forcing it round.

◀ Making woollen cloth was Britain's leading industry. Workers spun wool and wove cloth in their own homes. It was later taken to a *cloth finisher* like the one in this woodcarving in Spaxton Church in Somerset. You can see the tools he used. Holes show where the cloth was stretched tight on *tenterhooks* to dry after washing and cleaning.

Wool merchants joined together in guilds to stop other workers competing with them and to insist on common standards. The cloth merchants of Lavenham in Suffolk held their meetings in this fine *guildhall*. ▼

Windmills like this ▲ one, carved on a wooden bench in Bishop Lydeard Church, Somerset, turned the heavy round stones used to grind corn to make flour for bread.

LEISURE AND ENTERTAINMENT

Only the rich could afford to travel, so people spent holy days (holidays), such as Christmas or Easter, singing, feasting and dancing. Tudor sports and entertainments were noisy and often violent. Crowds of young men played football in the streets. Many took part in cruel sports, such as hunting, cock-fighting or watching dogs fighting dogs. Crowds attended the great fairs held in London and Cambridge.

At this wedding ▶ feast in Bermondsey, which was then a village outside London, the guests attend a feast and dance to music.

◀ This wooden stage at a village fair was like the London theatres where the plays of William Shakespeare were performed in the 1590s and early 1600s. They were open to the sky with a stage that jutted out into the middle of a courtyard. Most of the audience – known as the groundlings – stood below the stage in a sunken area called the pit. Rich people sat on chairs in galleries surrounding the stage.

John Evelyn ▶ described the frost fair held in London in January 1684. He 'went across the Thames on the ice' and was surprised to find it thick enough to support streets of shops, coaches, horses, cooks roasting meat over fires, as well as people on sledges and skates.

24

RELIGION AND SCIENCE

After Henry VIII broke away from the Roman Catholic Church, headed by the Pope, he named himself as Head of the Church in England. When the nine-year old Edward VI came to the throne in 1547, Britain was turned into a Protestant country. Mary I succeeded Edward in 1553 and tried to make the country Catholic again. She had Protestant *martyrs* who opposed her burned at the stake. Five years later, Elizabeth I cancelled Mary's laws but refused Puritan demands to get rid of everything connected with the Catholic Church. During her reign (1558-1603) and that of James I (1603-25), Catholics and Puritans alike were *persecuted.* Catholics were tortured and executed and some Puritans, such as the Pilgrim Fathers, sailed to America to start a new life.

Cardinal Wolsey, the powerful leader of the Catholic Church in Britain in the 1520s, lost favour with Henry VIII after the quarrel with the Pope and the Catholic Church.

Henry VIII annoyed ▶ many Roman Catholics when he had the **Latin** Bible translated into English. Queen Elizabeth I went even further, making the **Church of England** very different from the Roman Catholic Church.

The greatest of the Stuart scientists was Sir Isaac Newton. He thought up the law of gravity after watching an apple fall to the ground and he invented this reflecting telescope to help him study the planets. The telescope uses a mirror to help magnify the image of the stars. ▼

▲ Sir Christopher Wren designed the new St Paul's Cathedral after the Great Fire of London. It was very different from the old Catholic cathedral and had a great dome instead of a tower. Wren was also a distinguished scientist and a founder member of the Royal Society, which was set up in 1660 to help scientific research.

WARFARE

When Henry Tudor defeated Richard III at the Battle of Bosworth Field in 1485, castles were still being built and soldiers fought mainly with weapons such as pikes and bows and arrows. By 1714, wars were fought with guns and gunpowder and castles were a thing of the past.

◀ This Tudor fort was built at Deal in Kent to defend the coast of Britain against attack. Instead of arrowloops (narrow slits in the walls) from which to fire bows and arrows, it had gun holes through which the gunners inside the fort used to fire their *cannon*.

This Tudor cannon – Queen Elizabeth's ▶ Pocket Pistol – is on display at Dover in Kent, the nearest British port to Calais. It was later used by both *Roundhead* and *Cavalier* soldiers in the English Civil War.

The Spanish king sent a large army in a ▲ fleet of *galleons* and other warships to invade England in 1588. The Armada reached Calais harbour in France unharmed, but the sailors panicked when they saw flames from English *fireships* sailing towards them at night. The Armada split up and, under constant attack from English ships, returned to Spain round northern Scotland in a terrible storm which wrecked half the fleet.

England in 1500 was not as powerful as France or Spain. 200 years later Britain took a leading part in a war against France. The Duke of Marlborough, commanding a British and Allied army, won a series of stunning victories. Here he is, leading his men to victory at the Battle of Blenheim in 1704. ▼

GLOSSARY

Cannon A heavy gun mounted on wheels.

Cavaliers The supporters of King Charles I during the English Civil War.

Church of England The name of the Protestant church formed in England after the country broke away from the Catholic Church.

Civil war A war fought between people from the same country.

Cloth finisher The craftworker who cleaned the dirty, raw cloth woven by handloom weavers and turned it into a roll of cloth ready for sale.

Farthingale A hoop worn under a dress in the Elizabethan period to spread the skirt out.

Fireship A small ship without a crew, laden with firewood, and deliberately set on fire so that the wind pushed it towards the ships of an enemy fleet.

Galleon A huge sailing ship built in the Tudor period with three or more masts.

Guildhall The headquarters of a guild. This was an association of merchants, traders or craftworkers.

Latin The language spoken by the Romans.

Lord Protector The name taken by Oliver Cromwell to describe his position as ruler of Britain.

Martyrs People who were tortured and put to death because they refused to give up their religious beliefs.

Mullioned windows Windows made up of many tiny panes of glass with vertical supports (called mullions) separating the main panes.

Persecution This is when a group of people who share a common characteristic or interest (such as skin colour, language, race, or religion) are hunted down or harassed by their enemies.

Plague Bubonic plague was a deadly disease carried by flea-infested black rats which raised lumps on the patient called buboes.

Protestant A type of Christianity, opposed to some or all of the ideas or practices of Roman Catholics, which was founded in Europe in the sixteenth century.

Puritans Extreme Protestants who wanted to 'purify' the Church of England by ridding it of any ceremonies and practices similar to those in use in the Catholic Church. Puritans thought people should live simple lives.

Quoins The alternating rectangular and square blocks of stone at the corners of the walls on Stuart buildings.

Roundheads The name given to the supporters of Parliament during the English Civil War. It refers to the short hairstyle worn by some of the Roundhead soldiers.

Ruff A stiff round collar, usually made of lace or white cotton, which was gathered up into tucks, pleats or folds, and worn by fashionable men and women in the sixteenth and early seventeenth centuries.

Tenterhooks Hooks on a frame called a tenter, which was used to stretch wet cloth and stop it shrinking and losing its shape as it dried out.

IMPORTANT DATES

1485 Henry Tudor becomes the first of the Tudor monarchs after defeating and killing King Richard III at the Battle of Bosworth Field

1558 Elizabeth I (daughter of Anne Boleyn) becomes queen

1577 Sir Francis Drake sails round the world

1587 Execution of Mary, Queen of Scots

1603 Death of Queen Elizabeth I. James VI of Scotland becomes the first Stuart king as James I of England and Wales

1605 Gunpowder Plot foiled. Guy Fawkes arrested and later hanged.

1625 Charles I becomes king

1642 Start of the English Civil War between the armies of the king (the Cavaliers) and those of Parliament (the Roundheads)

1649 Trial and execution of King Charles I. England becomes a republic – a country without a monarch

1660 Charles II is restored to the throne as king after a period of chaos following the death of Cromwell

1685 James II, a Roman Catholic, becomes king

1688-9 King James II is deposed by Protestant forces loyal to Parliament and William III and Mary II succeed to the throne

1702 Anne becomes queen

1714 Death of Queen Anne

BOOKS TO READ

Here is a selection of books which can help you to build up a picture of life in the Tudor and Stuart period.

A Sixteenth Galleon by Richard Humble (Simon and Schuster, 1993)

Costume in Context: The Stuarts by Jennifer Ruby (Batsford, 1988)

Costume in Context: The Tudors by Jennifer Ruby (Batsford, 1989)

Craft Topics: Tudors by Rachel Wright (Franklin Watts, 1993)

How It Was: Elizabethan Life by Stewart Ross (Batsford, 1991)

Everyday Life in Stuart Times by Laurence Taylor (Simon and Schuster, 1993)

Everyday Life in Tudor Times by Haydn Middleton (Simon and Schuster, 1993)

Gunpowder, Treason and Plot by Lewis Weinstock (Wayland, 1987)

History in Evidence: Tudor Britain by Tony D Triggs (Wayland, 1989)

History Insights: Stuarts by Donna Bailey (Hodder and Stoughton, 1993)

History Insights: Tudors by Donna Bailey (Hodder and Stoughton, 1993)

How It Was: Tudor Monarchs by Jessica Saraga (Batsford, 1991)

INDEX

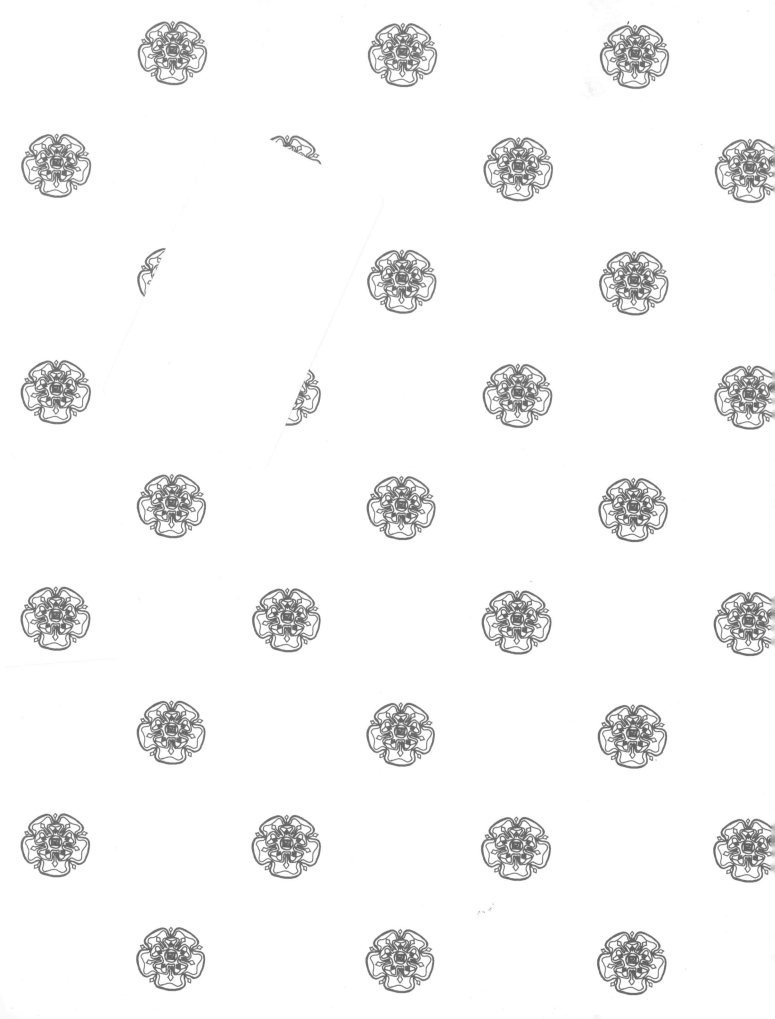